Surface Fugue

Surface Fugue

ISBN 978-1-934894-66-8

BOOK & COVER DESIGN: EK Larken

COVER IMAGE: Kenny Hurtado

Published by

EASTOVER — PRESS —

Rochester, Massachusetts
www.eastoverpress.com

Surface Fugue

poems

RALPH SNEEDEN

Praise for *Surface Fugue*

In Ralph Sneeden's remarkable second book of poems, *Surface Fugue*, the poet's descriptive attentions are so acute as to deftly and inexorably lead us into "a world we couldn't see," a world that lies "fathoms" below the surface of experience, or where "A wave's wall/ is the surface/ on its side." As a small-craft sailor and year-round surfer, Sneeden knows how to read the patterns and features of water and, from those shifting runes governed by planetary forces, discovers a sublime and buoyant joy that produces what he modestly but fiercely calls the "Elation/ of contact." The beautiful, dark, discursively in-gathering title poem, which finds in the relationship of prey and predator a metaphor for human greed, demonstrates that Sneeden is writing with a rare urgency and at the height of his powers.

—MICHAEL COLLIER, author of *The Ledge* and *Dark Wild Realm*

Surface Fugue reads like an extended lyrical meditation on family inheritances, the impact of war imagery and its metaphysical translations, a lesson on how beach walks can become transcendent exercises. Like a musician who has spent months in his woodshed, Sneeden emerges with brilliant variations on distance and memory, distillations of history and love, a sublime mix of self-reflection and intimacy juxtaposed with a larger world view. His approach to imagery, form, prosody and prose is so acute, tender, insightful and confrontational that a softball becomes a grenade and a photograph becomes a template for our psychic omissions. You are in the presence of a poet who understands that in order to parse a life and trace the steps to identity, a scar needs to be exposed before it can begin to heal.

—WILLIE PERDOMO, author of *The Crazy Bunch*

Beginnings of good stories involve strangers meeting on a lonely road, Ralph Sneeden tells us, but in his poems so much more is happening than just two humans meeting at an unlikely place: their memories also meet. This is because Sneeden is a master of making lyrics where memory reveals its mysterium, its engine, and so we open the book, see boys bike to school through the 1970s, a squall of yellowjackets pour down a child's throat, bike tires dip in the ochre ink of June's pollen. And, when we think we understand this poet's vision, he surprises us with pastures cropped by centuries of sheep. Surely, we realize right away that we are reading a poet with an unusual talent for making his remembered world into a place a reader can wander into and be stunned. Surely, there is something magnetic about Sneeden's singing aloud of experience. Surely, this writing is an act of spell-making. Yes. But it is also *so* take-no-prisoners real, *so* of *this* world, *so* needled with humor and heart, *so* full of tax returns and U-boats and tow trucks, that even skeptics among us will stand up defenseless. Which is to say: I love how Sneeden marries this world to wonder, how he asks not just what memory is, but what our kids' memories will be. I love how always—for this poet of New England—the geography his poetry takes and makes is all the beaches of New England, yes, but also of the mind. Bravo!

—ILYA KAMINSKY, author of *Dancing In Odessa* and *Deaf Republic*

for Gwen, Jake, Mads, and Eliza

and for Paul Yoon

and in memory of Andy Lindsay, voyager
1956-2020

Contents

Skiff Hill

Scars across this "sharpening rock"
(Nauset people honing tools
and weapons) would seem a glacier's striations,
if they didn't run like talon slashes
counter to the grain, didn't have
the texture of intention
                        instead of time.
A tourist's bench, now, with vistas
of the marshes where Champlain took it all
in—wild grape, beach plum, crops
of corn, pumpkin—decades before
the *Mayflower* (hunting the Hudson) spun
across trench and filigree, the Cape's
chronic wrist and forearm, shattered
elbow. In Chatham, his plaque classifies
...explorer, navigator, mapmaker, journalist,
artist and soldier.
                Where is the middle
distance of history?
              (Is it true
that massive plates from Vietnam, leftover
metal pads for chopper landing
skids, have been sunk vertically
like cultivar blades, integrated patches
in the border wall?)
              Nearly a mile
of *spartina* between voracious surf
and this bluff. Improbable that
whoever drew an axe-head down
this groove, stone to fashion stone,
would have mistaken those cones of sumac
berries for cardinals,
                tattered meat.

Refugees

Neither the squall of yellowjackets pouring
down my throat, nor the worker leaping
from backhoe to hoist and bear me from the log
I'd flipped for salamanders. Nothing remembered. All
related years later…like that rattlesnake beneath
the swings my father severed with a rake.
                            To forget
what must have been such pain and fear. Easy
as missing a belt loop; good friends
will point it out discreetly. Or, it comes back
on its own, a kettle whistling from another
room, when one has traveled from the origin,
creating distance as if it were a conscious art . . . .

A half century past the Chrysler's dwarfing
seat, grind of tires on the shoulder's gravel,
my grandfather cutting the engine so he could die.

Sometimes I wonder if the strutting gulls,
having flown so far inland, recall
the storm that drove them to these puddled fields
where they wander between the soccer goals,
bored, disoriented, until suddenly wheeling
their dutiful helix into the salty rain.

Meditation

I spent too much
time in Catholic churches
and hockey rinks and can't

nail why the two
conspire so in memory,
only that each evokes

a dread I used to think
was awareness of time being
wasted, time not spent

outdoors but inside, embalmed
with boredom and incense, or anxiety
in that meat locker mist

through which I skated
chasing down a puck
behind the net. Yes,

in those wars something
subtly exhilarating abided
the benches. Helmeted among

the steaming shoulders, I counted
the Zamboni's final laps,
new surface they promised

not unlike the mass's
hoped-for end, the day
beyond its babbling space,

its gestures, smoke, bells
and whistles, familiar rituals
of boys damaging boys,

men damaging boys
and men, men in uniforms
or robes, protecting men.

Physical Fitness

The awards I received in both fifth and sixth grades were signed by Richard Nixon. Or at least it was a picture of his signature. I knew he was reviled, but still I coveted that parchment in its red construction paper sheath and preserved as best I could the striking cloth patches (gold Presidential Eagle/field of blue) I never had my mother sew to the shoulders of my favorite windbreakers or sweatshirts. These were the early '70s and though we sacrificed two weeks of gym class to stop watches and tape measurers, there was nothing in those timed sprints or the distances we leapt across pits of grit to suggest that somewhere hundreds of thousands of people were being vaporized or shot by tens of thousands of our soldiers before they *themselves* were killed. Recently, I had Christmas dinner with a doctor who'd grown up in Vilnius in the '80s and every race he grunted or chin-up toward which he wrenched himself had as its goal the defeat of the army they were certain would invade. When I threw the softball down the field and the yards were counted and shouted back, we were not calculating if I could have reached with my best toss a bunker crammed full of Vietcong. My new friend the aspiring pediatric cardiothoracic surgeon heaved tennis balls filled with sand—to approximate the weight of grenades— at plywood dummies of American tanks. Everyone (he explained over Shiraz and standing ribs) would know the exact height of the sweet spot soft underbelly slot in the armor. "As children," he said, "we had been taught to recognize the place where our efforts might do the most damage."

An Azalea Blooms in the Murderer's Yard

And shirtless boys fire rocks with rackets
from the lawn next door. *Ping* and *twang*,
then sounds of invisible tunnels torn
through the canopy of indifferent oaks.

Perhaps it was them I saw, the scoundrels,
casting their lures in the middle of February,
hoping to snag the swans parked at the rim
of the flooded bog's unfreezing pupil.

He shot his family with a .22
not long after debarking the bus from school—
the quiet campus photographer, always
in the darkroom, it was said, waiting

for the images he'd abducted from the world
to unfurl in their shallow toxic pans.

Triptych: Portrait at Fifteen With Dog Swimming in Foreground

Whoever stopped rowing
took this picture of me
standing, fists in jacket
pockets, beside the rotting
pier, another potential
failure, feature of the empty
April beach, new
companion to surviving cedars
(that '30s hurricane), lone
forsythia, wry expositor,
its natural shape volcanic,
erupting.

        Kalimérisma—imploring
chant Greek women
offered earthbound for the waterborne,
fisherman and immigrants alike,
stroking out to net *lavráki*,
or sailing in from Maghreb.
The confused, looping meters
of pestle and oar.

        Subtle
wake, whirlpools trail
the loyal animal, whose snout's
orbit stirs the cove's
obscurity. I was trying
to whistle her back to shallows
believing she could distinguish
the chromatic melodies of welcome
from departure, beckoning from
lament, that she wouldn't follow
that stern until she sank,
but return to where I waited,
roll in sand then shake
the memory from her pelt.

from *Crab Studies:* Uca Pugnax (Fiddler Crab)

—after Ruskin and Van Gogh

Everything we wanted to know
was like chasing the light
inside a fridge, crouched

behind our scrim of *spartina*
waiting for that glimpse, the sand
suddenly coming alive

in concert—another conversation
we couldn't hear. Their hole-
openings filled with themselves,

those pathetic bodies, disproportionate
claws. Hours we spent
panicking to pry them out

after they retreated as one,
ramming our fingers down
their perfectly augered hallways,

dreading the moment of contact.

The Narrows: Lake George, 1969

We camp in a vise of mountains, *Black*
and *Erebus* answer the Tongue Range
with laughter, hatchet and paddle stroke

echoing the Mohawks en route to torch
Lachine, three centuries elapsed.
July, the first troops withdraw

from Vietnam. Our transistor
buzzes Armstrong's annexation of the moon,
its foil-wadded antenna-tip

twitching in lake-wind, ferried ghosts
of oak-fires, narration of wavelets rasping
granite. The stove's blue crowns

boil coffee to follow the meal
we've shared with the neighboring site:
immigrants, whose father, shot in the shoulder

(Budapest, '56), shows us his scar
by the light of the lantern. Our own, barely
twenty-five years past

a Baltic prison camp, his cheekbones
in mantle-glow, conjures the fort-swapping
French and British, Americans laying

siege, yarns of armies threading
that tired archipelago, bottleneck of history
corked with Fenimore Cooper's counterfeit

Indians: *Uncas, Chingachgook.* The other
self-effacing islands: *Phantom,*
Refuge, Little Recluse, As-You-

Were, Little As-You-Were.

Beach Walk, 1972

—for Matt Miller

Focused on unraveling high tide's
trashy embroidery, we foraged ahead, doubled
back to our dad in the morning game he
devised to keep us busy. He'd waited out
the War's last spasms in a German camp.
Now, he kicked driftwood, toed a fish spine,
stopped to study the bay or bend with us
for whelk, limpet, "mermaid's fingernail,"
violet mussel-pearl, lost lures
with talons tangled in rusty monofilament,
their painted eyes inscrutable. The rare seahorse,
poignant to find one brittle, dead. Generous
praise when we held up what was left
of bottles drowned in boat wakes, scuffed buttons
of *Bud* or *Ballantine,* green of *Seven-Up*
punctuating the ubiquitous aqua of shattered *Cokes,*
some of which he made us sling reluctantly
beyond the reach of waders' feet, surrendered
to another winter's grinding, to the sort of gray
sea a parent would scan for traces of a child's
flight, the girl whose wings beat to leave
our kitchen counter's magazine. Naked on a runway
of pain, herded by GI's, racing a wall
of smoke, a little Icarus whose labyrinth had just
begun, scavenging survival instead of hoping
for explosion from the seaweed's olive pods.
We'd found the real thing nesting among
the panicles, too, fifth of July's damp
cylinders we pocketed, forgot. Later that week,
with the shells' laundered nacre, flecks of fire-
cracker paper like down in the dryer's lint trap.

Boys Playing Army in a Deserted Nursery
—for Dave Smith

...the agony of citizenship is never ending
—Roger D. Hodge

We taunted the ram in his paddock; he butted us back
to the bleached tinder of last year's rye
where we flicked matches, whacked chains of charred

patches with team jackets while April egged
the smolders we couldn't see, stretched flames
as mothers might a sheet across the abdicated

mattresses, from one pasture's bevy of coddled
birches to another's rhododendrons, weeping
hemlocks entwined in stunted hamlets. Empty expletives

of smoke were already being scoured from clouds
above the rows of failed rebellion, so
we ran to the future, regret an ember to resuscitate

along the turnpikes, embarked for the adversaries, pushing
computer mice, vacuums, and suffering daily
the subway gate's punctual insult, cold

metal irreversible against our groins.

Rhodesia

The idea of being a mercenary appealed to me in junior high. Oh, I skydived through that canopy like an olive drab dart, rattling with gunmetal, all bandolier and camo, into imagined backwater kingdoms for nothing but swashbuckling loyalty to myself, playing army, getting paid for doing anonymous harm in the name of causes for which I couldn't muster any language, only a dim comprehension of transactions with aloof attachés who coyly underwrote my exploits.

Adolescence, extinct quagmire, decolonized fantasy, why this recon back to your spectral borders, your name replaced within that decade, little Rhodesia of the mind, subsumed state I invaded, occupied, shot up, outgrew? O obsolete classroom globes, fucked-up euphemisms! *Freedom Fighters, Mercs.* BE A MAN AMONG MEN blared red from my favorite tee: white, ten bucks, back pages, *Soldier of Fortune* magazine. (Milton's riff, recognized when college chucked it to the oil-smeared beaches of my phony adulthood like an empty vodka bottle with its crumpled calligraphic plea, the Almighty to his Son, "…be thyself a man among men on earth.")

And that beret I bought from Jerry's Army/Navy, while my dad pored over tarps and rope. Wrong size, no insignia or country of origin, played-out leather band stretched around my skull as I cantered on the mower's saddle massacring the leaves around our house, earning the cash to order that stupid shirt. Inside, my benefactors balanced their checkbooks, waxed the floors, built bookcases to support our failing province of Britannica, and would have, most likely, when confronted by neighbors, denied ever knowing me.

The New Bathymetry

On the photo, "Children Bathing, 1947"
—Charles "Teenie" Harris

Summer relief was different for us:
playing Cousteau in another galaxy,
relinquishing our makeshift grappling

hook (broken rake) when it snagged
a mooring chain, the brave among us
diving, eyes clamped, kicking

downward to plunge forearm deep
into muck for who knows what.
At school we'd seen beneath the ocean's

infinity; filmstrips erased reflection,
filtered murk of fathoms to reveal
the continent's continuation. We understood

where we stood was just our slab's
extension; without water, we could stroll
to basalt basements, the Marianas Trench,

and find what we'd always suspected yet
denied without a way of being
part. So, what am I searching for

in these faces under a Pittsburgh hydrant's
sidewalk storm? Why this need
to superimpose my own, or even venture

that they're studying future selves with a kind
of enigmatic dignity, imagining other
people pinned to bricks by hose jets?

We crowded the gunwale, drawing our perforated
bucket up, its plume of silt
in the sunshot green a suddenly redolent,

fecal glyph smearing the prow, which,
once the sand was under our feet,
we rinsed with a handful of Atlantic.

Fish Brook

And yet, off alone, we were happy
with what stayed the same, and we stood there
in the space between world and plaything,
upon a spot which, from the beginning.
had been established for pure event.
                    —*Rilke, from "The Fourth Elegy"*

Beneath the highway, the stream was wide and shallow. Cars and trucks
hammered overhead, a pattern to their muted thwacking of potholes like the
pop of a snare drum where the bridge's metal seams joined pavement, echoes
almost compatible with the hiss of water rushing over gravel where I was
standing, all of it suddenly obliterated by the staccato growl and diminishing
roar of an eighteen-wheeler's compression brake, a chapel divebombed by
electric guitars.

I was thirteen, wading Fish Brook from its source at the Mill Pond, a short,
one-handed bike ride from my house, rod cocked like a lance. Even then, the
mill had been defunct for decades, still withdrawing as planks collapsed around
the pitted metal of its protruding circular blade like a skull around its jaw
and single tooth. But flowing from that ruin, the brook fulfilled its promise. I
was good at coaxing browns and rainbows out of hiding, positioning myself
upstream to drift a weightless tatter of earthworm just under the bank.

Driving through Massachusetts on route 95, I can't pass the small sign with the
name of the stream without remembering the many drivers I imagined going
about their weekend business on a hot Saturday in May of 1973, unaware of
the boy in cut-off jeans and canvas sneakers poised beneath them in the center
of the current, praying to the tip of his fishing rod. Because they can't see him,
they have no way of knowing that he is down there wondering what to worry
about. The war is almost over, the draft along with it. His parents have been
floating the idea of a part-time job, which almost seems as ominous as the
prospect of military service, his college-age sisters' summers already begun,
waiting tables at a Howard Johnson's a mile up the highway, pumping gas on
the Cape. Lately, his reverie is being worn down by something permanent,
something immune to ceasefires, with no regard for Peace Talks. Until today,
it has been easy for him to keep his senses tuned to the chase, the adventure
of following that snaking course to arrive at some mysterious green pool that
might take his breath away. He has never followed it this far and considers
whether the fish themselves are aware of or care about the contrivance of the

tunnel, a passage built to convince the brook (and them) that nothing had really changed. But the motorists above seem as oblivious, so he'll never be someone else's memory, his adolescent ghost nowhere in their minds when they are older, the many sources of their own anxieties already come to pass, like his, as they hurtle past this spot through time, like me.

My first stereo came from the company store—General Electric, famous for appliances, though what my father did was design an engine for a jet that was really a flying Gatling gun. (The A10 Thunderbolt, a.k.a. "Warthog," now on the verge of retirement, can pound a tank to foil with one burst: 4,200 armor-piercing, depleted uranium rounds per minute.) These were the early, heady days of *components*, speakers weaned from phonographs, sent like brats to board on living room bookshelves a safe distance from parental turntable, power of the amp. On my birthday that spring, he'd brought it home in one box, surrendered without the provisions of my Christmas BB gun, though volume from my bedroom could dispatch chickadees from backyard birches as efficiently. My sisters had already opened our front door to The Doors and let in Led Zeppelin, Iron Butterfly, too, who, by the weight of their names, had no business being airborne in our home, power chords overlapping abrasive vapor trails in a dogfight with my father's brass (the Dorseys, Miller, Getz) and my own insurgent metallurgy (Deep Purple, Uriah Heep) scrambling its fleet.

He'd taken me with him to the Plant, to the wind tunnel where testing had recently put a turbine through its paces, and he conferred with clipboard technicians, and the machine cooled on its mount like a woofer ripped from a speaker, creature from its shell. Finished shooting turkey carcasses through its howling fan, they hunched over data, calculating how many birds an engine could ingest in flight before it failed. Bored and doodling, I waited in the soundproof glass booth, sterile terrarium, observed my dad doing what he did to put sweatshirts on my back, hockey pads on my shoulders and shins, a *Daiwa* reel on my rod and lasagnas on our kitchen table downstairs from the room where I could play my music without having to listen to anything else, impervious to the cacophony necessary for the study of limits.

That subterranean stretch of Fish Brook—an engineered space below a road that went from Maine to Miami, earth coaxed by bulldozers, rebar and concrete colluding in a corridor of water, major highway for a roof—was no place to be fishing. In the reflected gray half-light, I played out my line through the cage of rays skewering down through the median's openings. Where my tackle drifted was just a guess. What I preferred was the musky shade of hemlock banks guiding a deeper but seductively luminous current, the looping furrow it carved through bright grasses in an old sheep pasture, past eroded overhangs, the exposed and mortified roots of oaks.

Before I emerged to glance back at the traffic, those lives I'd been hearing but couldn't see, the tunnel opening hovered ahead like a waning planet spied through backward binoculars, an entire world compressed and animated in the newly minted leaves of swamp maples waffling impatiently in sunlight just beyond the abutment.

Children Driving

The tide flew from them as far
as the planet permitted. Abandoning asphalt,
they headed straight for sea-glazed flats,
dispersing gulls in a father's borrowed
pickup, that game of dodging driftwood
stumps and lurching suddenly to softer
sand. Waves would return to drown
their swerves, the pall of salt and marsh stink
to supplant the angry exhaust from all
their revving until the axles were buried.

When the names of roads began to matter,
towns, like boats adrift, found their ports,
moorings. Sadness arrived with orientation,
with exile from being conveyed all their lives
through a world of destinations only arrived
a burden. That the coast was *west* or sun
deflated there, or all that traffic was herding
north mattered as much as rent, the price
of cereal, socks. Numbers now found
traction astride a restaurant's neon cactus,
giant stucco duck, or rusting bridge
across an unpronounceable river.

Driving Past the Properties
I Landscaped as a Teenager

Look, netted in shadows of dying
elms, we study our sandwiches like manuals,
unscrew thermos warheads, doze,

hat brims down, while one cups a joint
as if it were a hatchling, offering
cinder and smoke, a rope flung

to where I toil astride this trough
of what I never want to set,
drydocked boat of wet cement

I'm sculling with a spade across
the centuries to myself. Yew
and aster obscure the true artistry:

holes. And all those acres of groomed
and sifted loam, censored by sod
that is always chafing like green

surf the terraced nostalgia for backaches,
bedrock, impenetrable soil, for being
on my knees again with a mallet,

tamping the puzzle of herringboned brick
or coaxing grit between the cobbles
of paths that were never mine to take.

Language

My college girlfriend read
her other boyfriend's poems
to me one night, some
graduate student who drove
from Boston on weekends, whose name
was George, because of which
he somehow seemed more
literary than I. I
remember some conceit
about maps: the routes
through their time together,
how he strode along
the "blue turnpikes" of her veins
with his tanned fingers,
etc. She must have loved them
(the poems); they were for her,
but suddenly offered to me
as if *her* own, written
for *me*. They were. My
humiliation probably not
what she was after, nor praise
for my rival. We leaned
against each other like lovers,
though we weren't, really,
(some dead aunt's couch
bandaged in afghans, weed-smoke).
Once, I met them back
from one of their hikes, absorbed
his praise of trailside grapes:
"…pungent, intoxicating." *What
people use this language?*
I thought, standing bathed in
the florescent corpse-light of the dorm's
hallway, its tangled, stubborn
smells, our brands of deodorant
and beer, limited, identifiable.

Frozen Boat

Hardy knew the beginnings of good
stories involve two strangers meeting
on a lonely road. That's the way

it seems finding the green lobster boat
locked in ice, one hull sticking out
winter, prow aligned to eastern

light which rushes the inlet, aspiring
tide. The fragile craft designed
for *pleasure* hauled and wrapped

months ago, along with their puns,
vain language of their witty rumps.
The only words now a name, arched,

indecipherable below a single transom.
The way we live, it's always *work*
that makes us somebody—rust stains,

mud-smear, gunwales worn to grain
by the rhythm of retrieval, expectation,
stuffing mesh bags with foul carcasses

intended to draw the hungry and listless,
to change their foraging lives for good
beneath the bright buoys of ownership.

Boys Riding Bicycles to School

—In Memoriam, T. P.

They're always pedaling up the long hill
from 1970, standing upright on their pedals
to trace with careless penmanship, tires
dipped in the ochre ink of June's pollen,
our confused directions from one decade
to the next.
             Leaves have barely unfurled
above the antlers of weaving handlebars,
rusted chains and rims, and still they ignore
commuters' honks as they have all
those reminders, that nagging not to leave
things in the rain.
               Perhaps the impossible cool
of hemlocks is where they've been, abandoned
nursery where they hunkered in depressions
of extracted maples, dropping acid, waiting
for the precision-guided future…
                  Spin on,
oblivious gyroscopes. It is your last day
of classes. And because everything is ending, you
have never been as enthusiastic to reach it.

Tunnel, Regent's Canal

All cabin, recklessly invested in interior,
the barges barely accommodate the nostalgia
of their potted plants, anxious immigrants, committed
pragmatists crowding the round prows; they're on
their own—the geraniums, grape hyacinths—have been
for some time, revving but resentful. It's March
around this rainbow raft of caskets, each
with an umbilicus of arm-thick IV's
snaking the ivied terraces, bound for the throbbing
reservoirs, electricity.
                   O *Lavender Jewel,*
Grub... Who can recall the crimes that got you
here, the combinations to unfetter these rusting bikes
from your railings? I wish I'd met the revelers
who killed the magnum cradled in its bucket
before the label peeled away and this wedge
of rain moved in. Perhaps they cast their lines,
considered communion with this hole in the heart
of London where signs encourage us to imagine
voyagers deep inside a practice Avernus
and, should they emerge, surrender the right of way.

Here is where we idle near the entrance,
pretend to mull infinity from the ranks
of the unaffiliated, hum our earthbound barcarole,
no chance of collision, trading gunwale paint
with whoever's coming back the other way,
boat stoves oozing peat smoke, acrid warmth
rising to join everything else's exhalations:
purposeful diesel, espresso, sweet hookahs,
guano of the netted park's neglected aviaries.

Prayer as Bomb

O delayed fuse, O bloated roadside dog,
corroded mine. Let the undetonated salvos
sleep entombed in coral. Snuff the yolk
of those abandoned eggs, their deep insinuations
beneath the fields of necessary grain. Open
the bay, bury us with a blizzard of whistling
postcards, all our demands RETURNED TO SENDER.
You'll find us in pieces, quivering in the craters
or emerging from a bus's smoldering statement,
having forgotten (but gotten what we deserved)
why it was we stepped across this threshold
with whatever hope it was we'd strapped
so deliberately, meticulously to ourselves.

Litus Saxonicum

—after reading a tourist pamphlet by Leonard Cottrell,
published by Her Majesty's Stationery Office, 1964

The occupied were once rapacious, too. The past
is like matter; you see its forgery in prisoners'
bored inscriptions (Seven Years War),
a cannon's Tudor rose, embossed. Churchill's
pillboxes never shake their Centurions, pear-shaped
bastions their Middle-Aged flab. Excavating
the indiscretions, engineers snap drill-bits
at *Branodunum* and *Rutupiae* (Brancaster, Richborough).
Easier to punctuate stone than that stubborn cement.

Roman Forts of the Saxon Shore: tribal
tussle with time for a quick dip in meter's
troughs, the muted pools of vowels between
capitals that flutter like languid pennants at river-
mouths, fringed umbrellas at eroding beachheads.

Elegy: Letter to My Wife's Grandfather, Canadian Artillery, 1917

Ambrose, that sea beyond the white
Perbeck stone in Dorset was not
unlike the sky above the ossuary

at Verdun. Pastures cropped by centuries
of sheep, as familiar underfoot
as a military cemetery's velvet

green. The grass's secret of self-
preservation: keeping its head
down, growing *out*, not up.

Hardy's cottage was in a cage
of scaffolding. At his desk we squinted
behind bars, pretended to see

foxgloves as he had, but framed by the apparatus
of repair; because the foundation was sunk
in sand, the walls were pulling away.

This was after our pilgrimage of thanks
for your surviving Arras, the flu
that kept you in a cot and off

of Vimy Ridge, carnage that caught
up with your heart at fifty-five,
a family doctor taking eggs

from patients instead of money. A detour
in Agny at Edward Thomas's grave,
the poet whose sadness made him walk,

whose love of England's roads was impetus
enough for enlisting at thirty-eight,
lighting his pipe when a shell stopped

his heart with its passing and like a blessing
left no marks. Uneasy picnic
sitting on the bumper, shaggy

coast of meadow we'd driven across
to reach the shorn island. Maintenance,
I guess, is respect, softens the stones'

inarguable dates. Stalks had clawed
the chassis like finger bones, a wire
brush or sand on a skiff's hull;

we'd run aground, marooned with mediocre
cheese, cheap red, olives,
bread, flotilla of apartments anchored

off the opposite shore, one
particular balcony like a departing stern,
someone at the railing punishing a rug,

dust apologizing across the sun.

Lewisham

Can't stop staring at that patch of newer brick where something tore a hole—souvenir, perhaps, of the V-1 that killed three hundred in a go. In '44, houses vanished overnight.

A quick, damp pedal under the Thames and you're in Greenwich, where the telescopes look like weapons, and where I'd learned the Meridian was a decision, and where I placed my palm against a meteorite: "The Oldest Thing on Earth."

(Relatively recently, French villagers learned the material quarried from neighboring hills had been one of these. Imagine the exasperated geologist trying to persuade them that the very walls behind which they'd broken bread, would breathe their last, and where ancestors hunkered through winters, occupations and pandemics for centuries…had come to them from space. They might have shrugged, *"Quelle est la différence?"* pausing between ripping fistfuls of feathers from a chicken's back. *"Un rocher est un rocher."*)

Beyond the observatory, up the hill, Blackheath—rumored to have been the largest burial pit during The Plague.

Midnight, walking from the train, I tracked the shadows of foxes jogging the jagged tops of garden walls, those tidy backyard partitions like roofless rooms, trying to picture the lone Saxon or Jute beaching in 600, who lurches as his prow rams silt. Who settles by burning his boat.

Giant Nazi Flag Escapes
From an Attic Vodka Box

My mother lets it out by accident,
mistaken for another crate of crap,
tax returns to shred. Standard

of a century's cruel alluvion,
as if pressed and folded yesterday,
poised for one more parade, no

moth holes, a flume-blade of cloth
to be dropped on the desperately complicit
or blot every arch's camber

and pigeon-thronged entablature,
instead of searing our ceiling
with pink light. A souvenir

my father never mentioned before
he died, unlike the snake of spurred
wire, public, mounted on its routed

plaque above his desk, memento
snipped that day of his deliverance
from the camp. The flag unfurls

from her fingers like a bolt
of oxygenated blood from catwalk
balcony to living room, rip

against the tidal bore of twilight
filling windows with the cove's
kleptocracy, that single heron

crimping an eel to heft it flailing
into the conflations of Autumn, over
the meager pockets of marshbank reflections

being siphoned of their last silver.

Two Short Films of My Father

I.

Liberation of Stalag Luft One: Barth, Germany, 1945
—for Ellen Bryant Voigt

Like any lyric, nothing happens;
a core fueled by something outside
the interminable moment—lines
of soldiers filing without origin,
that slow parade of boyish smokers
trudging rags of mismatched uniforms
and smirks toward but not into
the flank of a waiting plane. I trust
he is among them, have to watch
with the sort of faith his parents
mustered poring over censored
letters, longing between the lines,
bored evocations of boredom: he was
alive, but wasn't free. And we
never see them board the plane.
Like any narrative, it must be followed
for the purpose of learning what happens,
because something *does*. It has
already, yet it never can.

II.

En Route, Olympic Games: London, 1948

Whoever aims the camera struggles
to keep the horizon level. The ship
pitches, rights itself like the world
in which they've lived, a liner's cargo
of nervous men in uniform, going
overseas again. Scripted calisthenics
on the deck above the silent bow-
wave of black, hull-peeled water.
Cigarettes, self-conscious chatting,
elbows on the gleaming brightwork,
bangs lifting. And there, swinging
around his neck, the religious medal
he wore throughout the war and after.
In the tropics they told him to leave it
on the beach; flashing, it would only
lure the barracudas to his throat.
Though I didn't believe in the power
of its little saint I always
wanted one like it, silver pendant
to chafe the chests of all my tees,
wear holes my mother, in disgust,
would widen with her finger folding
laundry on their bed. A talisman
that might keep me from drowning,
or at least catch light through water
while I swam, like him, from shore.

The Cigarette Wheel:
Seaside Heights, New Jersey, 1942
—for my mother

At pier's end the coaster's warped spine
silent, deserted against the night. And black-
out curtains drawn along the boardwalk's frenzied
stage—ruse intermission, as if the play
went on while the ocean checked its watch.
Her job: to heave the arrow, call a number,
underhand toss the cartons to winners.

         Somewhere
out there in the darkness U-Boats hoped
to draw their beads on freighter shapes against
escaping light. Beneath her feet, determined
detonations, a chill between the planks
as pylons gutted breakers, people around her
hammering fists while the metal claw buzzed,
slowed to ticking, trapped between the pegs.

Search Engine

Maybe the priest who tried to seduce
my father during a marriage interview
was just lonely, horny, surviving
in his seminary like a spider in a jar.
I confess my sad numbness to the news
of serial pedophiles in the Church,
but an adult lured to a sauna
on his "tour" seems different. My dad,
the bomber pilot only five years
past two in a Nazi camp,
who gave up his early twenties, not
to mention teeth (to shitty food;
ditto, lungs to Luckys). Father/
Brother What's-His-Name must
be dead now, too, so it's mine,
this story, having been my mother's,
a memory that isn't ours. And the search
for sense yields an array of theories
why the priest embarked on this escapade
with an ex-POW. Hard to name exactly
what fueled such internal combustion,
self-loathing, what sparked
those pistons to action instead of yearning,
and my own yearning for results:
that culled herd of info stampeding
from the exponential oases, that brain-swarm,
apoplectic sortie vibrating in response
to bricks we lob at its gray inscrutable
hive. My dad, wondering how
a sauna was relevant to engagement or being
Catholic, felt the pressure of fingers
on his collarbone, spun to find
that dude without a stitch, as tactless
as the day he was born, bereft
of answers for the questions that came next.

San Fernando Valley, 1961

Punctual gods of my father's jet
propulsion tests lit up the San
Garbiels, counterfeit storms, deferred
call and response with flashbulbs ignited
to enshrine my sisters stooped beside
the concrete grotto in apathetic prayer—
Saint Mel's, newly sprung
among the silenced bucket loaders,
churned scrub, white and modern
as Apollo on the pad, cocked
with the sun in its crosshairs. Palm Sunday,
beltless in the back seat we knighted
and fanned each other, brandished the green
scepters with care, suspicion, their derivations
plunked in ranks to salute Ventura's
traffic, the horizon's fresh corrugations.
We blessed garages, sidewalk dogs,
a woman pumping sunburned arms,
frond gripped in her fist as if
to flog the surviving citrus rows
and beleaguered groves of walnut through
the canyon fog to exile, far from
split-rails, pickets, dependent roses.
We ranged in our finned wagon, fugitive
bougainvillea defecting from trellises,
window frames, adobe doorways
headlocked in horseshoes of purple fire.

from *Crab Studies:* Libinia Emarginata (Common Spider Crab)

—after Ruskin and Van Gogh

We cranked him upward clinging
to the hook, recognized the dead
weight, absence of fin-jerk

or frustrated muscle of captive's
shock. Distracted by fortune,
excavating our ribbon of pleated

squid, he didn't let go
until his back broke
the surface. Decades past

this instant, I remember
my father too often,
our bait intact and the ugly

crab dissolving as it sank
like a doomed theory or dream,
shaken, provisional, spindles

spread in the fathoms. Elation
of contact with something from
a world we couldn't see

soon supplanted by disgust,
relief: his self-liberation
saving us from the business

of extracting that hook ourselves.

Loss Prevention

Saying *theft* you must be prepared
to name a thief, whereas *loss*
suggests the seller's problem, owner's
fault, without accusing customers

before they have a chance to buy.
Trust me, the merchandise will find
another exit—in children's pockets,
sweaters migrating beneath other

sweaters—while escalators convey us
silently from each other's sight.
The services provided are not enough,
these stapled bags, initialed receipts.

Your meticulous gardens will be pillaged,
terraces between the generations washed
right down the slope (…the shelves of
my father's entire family emptied

so quickly while everyone seemed to look
the other way). How can we know
what Wordsworth, thirteen, taken
home from school to find himself

an orphan, felt? He described waiting
on the hill for his brothers' horses,
the sound of the wind, a stone-wall,
a sheep, stunted hawthorn tree.

Years later he waved farewell
to a brother descending the sunny path
along a stream, then lost that brother
to the sea. He fled one home because

the windows framed his children's graves.
His lake rarely freezes anymore.
Behind the glass his skates are sealed
like wizened bats. Scheduled embers

crackle on the grate. But spring threatens
the pantry flags, to lift with flood
the stores as it always has. Gluttonous
trout ascend from bridge-shadow

to crumbs the tourists drop within
eyeshot of his headstone, its black
hip-high iron pickets meant
to keep the living at a distance.

Elegy: Late August, Ipswich Bay

> Would now the wind but had a body.
> —*Melville*

Resign yourself, abandon other plans
when sailing; address distance by abandoning time.
Forget what you want to reach in order to arrive.

Forty years ago, he was alive.
We crossed the sound to camp here, sublime
until resigning ourselves, abandoning plans

when mosquitoes drove us from our tarp, the chance
to sleep to the rocking mast, its muted chime,
to forget. What we wanted: to reach. In order to arrive,

we'd tacked the estuary only to tack the sands,
walking the night, pivoting every time
we resigned ourselves to abandon our plans

of reaching the point, retracing our trail's scents
of camphor, canvas, woodsmoke's lazy climb,
forgetting what it wanted to reach in order to arrive

across the moon, whose light darkened our prints
with shadows enough to follow. Comfortable with the crime
of resigning ourselves, abandoning other plans,
we forgot what we wanted: to reach in order to arrive.

Orient Point

My father took too many pictures
of gulls—bored opportunists, nothing
but gray dollops on pilings, or bitching
as they stitched the air over the wake
behind us (lots of blossoms, too, contrasts
of warring storm clouds, cathedrals blurry
at night, and glaciers in Austria, receding,
probably vanished now).
                                        I remember
him chasing ferry tickets the wind
had stolen from his hand at the booth,
and that camera, black amulet flogging
his chest as he sprinted the beach away
from us, driver's door flung open,
empty seat, our mother all worked
up, shouting something about his heart.

Automotive

Impressed again by my knowledge
of cars—those late '60s/early
'70s grills, configuration and squint
of taillights classifiable as waterfowl.
That perfect facsimile of my uncle's Eldorado
listing like a float up 95,
same tilt of a Homburg's peak and brim
above the seatback—beguiling, ephemeral
as the other owners I'll never meet.
That sorry ragtop I dinged with my basket
in the market lot. Aqua shitbox, cheap
clone of a California beauty, WINDI
on its plate. I *liked* that song
and remember when that color topped
the charts then vanished with the same
physics that sucked my father's smoke
out the jib-shaped gill of his
Camaro's louvered window. In
a jam, I drum the dash behind
a tow truck and its ass-hooked, corroded soldier,
start the staring contest with its surviving
headlight, half-filled with rainwater,
brooding backward through traffic.

Asymptomatic

When masks are gone, my mother
wonders how our kids
will remember this era when
they are old, like her.
Take the vestiges of polio:
Had she been afraid for us,
watching from the kitchen
our babysitter limp back home,
vanishing through California
walnut trees? "Sort of,"
she says, likening it to the War's
proximity and threat, her own
adolescence of watching boys
ship out, return intact,
or without limbs, or not
at all. Same with the news
of protests, police killings,
a government drained by a tick.
It's as if she's summoning
the memory of a vague pal
from junior high: "Close
but not that close."

Shipyard Aubade

Everything evicted or planning escape.
The green water antiseptic, colder now,
if that's possible. Without a means of getting
out there to the boat, you have to swim,

October having culled the settlement to make
an example of the stubborn decks desecrated
by gulls' graffiti, devastated crabs. Always
risky to tempt this season, its barreling storms,

for one more shot at skirting the bay, unfurling
a sail to smother the marshes' threats of arson,
before you take it down for good, tide
nipping the lug bolts of your trailer waiting

on the beach, smug foresight of the empty
moorings, pert wrinkles of their little wakes,
the current you thrash against. To let your body
pass, a school of herring adjusts the obedient

contours of its involuntary, brilliant cause.

Outside

I can't get enough
of the swell's blunt barometric
news, hedging fatigue,
surfboard calipered between
my knees just outside
the threshold where waves genuflect
to beach and blow their lids.
      I love their predictable
histrionics before the sun
swings down from the rafters
of western clouds to take
his pot shots, flaming arrows
some breakers take straight
to their bared chests, trans-
planted molten hearts too
bloated to bear any distance.
      I'm still out here jabbering
to myself, sizing up
every gunmetal bus
of ocean powersliding through
my station, as light, the definer,
dims and with it the shadow
or glimmer required to read
the sheen for rides. Too spent
to paddle, recluse with a big
personality,
          always the last
misanthrope to leave the party.

After the Shark

People know me by what
has happened to me, not
what I have done. My deeds,
superimposed, almost hide
the residuum of the event,
but this does not prevent
me from cleaning the upturned
mower's blades by hand
or searching for the shattered
glass in the sink of water
opaque with soap and filth.
Friends commend my mirth
though they seek the damage,
the stamp of teeth, the badge
of my skin's history, the proof,
the rooms dismissed for the roof,
while I still imagine the blur
of whatever prowls the ether
of the reefs, thrusting appetite
before it, a banner bright
with the other unseized lives.
My own, forgotten, dissolves
in the particulate blue of hours,
their invisible wake. But power
relinquished is power gained;
devoured suggests the pained
freedom of being unsavored,
an unappreciated flavor,
whim incarnate, a waste
of time with immortal aftertaste.

Bathers at White Horse Beach

—after a photograph c. 1900

When light allows,
                 a dipping oar
is able to inhabit both worlds;
the bonus of refraction is surviving
the being severed.
              But she is dissolving
entirely into an ocean satisfied
with surface, private as mercury,
as deaf and complicit as the Tyrrhenian
Sea in Antonioni's *L'Avventura*,
his heroine calling out a name
to what could never answer.
                  Weston's
final shots at Lobos, too,
forensic, a record of throes, legions
of stillborn sculptures in the ledge,
rotting pelican, stagnant pool
and wheel of kelp like a galaxy's exo-
skeleton, a memory of light.
                  At centuries'
fulcrum, her bathing costume darkens,
absorbs the eddy, gray and swirling
at her knees. How many urns
since emptied to the undulations,
bodies mingling
            with detritus?
Fellini never stopped wondering
why patients in the asylum refused
clothing, swaddled themselves in garlands
unraveled from the mounds of pungent
seaweed forked to their cells,
                where I
imagine them pale, writhing like squid
tossed to the berm by October storms,
tentacles in gestures
           of propulsion.

Poem About Walden Pond Without Any Mention of Thoreau

The swim was a means of stripping
the patina of tourist's grime. Dust
sueded the leaves, hung over
the parking lot like cannon smoke,
packed gravel still trembling with
the decamped army, sated herd.
That day, I'd imagined enough
proof of revolution, a road quilled
with bayonets, seen the famous recon-
structed bridge, tracked (from the safety
of Emerson's arbor) a thunderstorm strafing
hills, all gunpowder and bilious
pewter.
      The pondwater was clean. Serious
swimmers in Lycra and goggles passed me
as if I were roadkill, trolling the freight
of torsos and legs in haphazard lanes.
It was then I considered the urban
refugees back in their walkups, sad
the chill of the dip had fled their skin
while cussing out a sun that wouldn't
quit. Too hot to cook, showered
and shirtless, were they firing up
their fans, shivering in the mist before
the plundered tombs of their freezers,
equivocating takeout? *Tacos? Mongolian
barbeque?*
      On my back, ditched
noncombatant angel, I gave up
lumbering up the ladder of thought-
over-thought from my buoyant self,
capsized, set my compass for *sink*
and stroked through the green fantasy
of getting to the bottom
                  of everything.

Wind Indicators

Six-inch lengths of tape
I cut from an old cassette
and knotted to the shrouds astride
the mast of this twelve-foot

leaking boat. I didn't care
to know the genre before I ripped
the entrails squealing from their hubs:
something dated, indecipherable

ballpoint on the label. Another phase
of life that's best forgotten,
put to better use. How primitive
the plastic box, its moving parts:

a ribbon read by magnet, fed
like grain across a millstone's molars.
You count on them to translate where
the wind is from, where it wants

to go. How certain I was
that my face or the confessions of traitorous
flags and trees on shore would be
enough. August, they're almost invisible,

the interrupted clips of sound
scoured by sun, ceaseless whipping—
frayed glimmers if the light
is right. Though, for months, brown

opacity painted on the tape
was music I could *see*, a couple
of beats, fragment of a bar, half
a riff writhing in the air that filled

the sail and blew me from the mooring.

Jacksonville Beach

Someone must watch, it is said. Someone must be there.
—*Kafka*

I should have blood on my hands instead
of time. Nothing at stake in my boredom
here, while lifeguards perch in hours
of scrutiny knowing the ratio will yield
at least one instance of struggle
or violence, inviting the intervention
they've trained for. I watch the Red Cross
recruits shoulder sandbags, surrogate
bodies (literal weight of the world)
yoking sunburned muscle. Their seniors
preside in stilted chairs, extending
meditation past that zone between
dangerous jade and inshore turbidity
where a bather girds, his wrist braceleted
by the chain of a swimming Pit Bull.

Shinkawa's Problem

I wonder if he loved the ocean
even more that day the tsunami
swept him and his cottage from the soil
then miles out, a wave with arms
like a victor's raking back
the chips. So many afternoons,
the Pacific had kept its blunt ontologies
from him, offshore winds denying
effervescence, stealing tang. Kelpy
musk ignored by open windows,
and the fog, too, quarantined to its violet
cities on the horizon,
                            among which suddenly
he squatted on roof-shingles, days of pondering
the destruction he couldn't see, though what
had wrought it was all around and nowhere,
hit-and-run guardian angel
fled before he could thank it for leaving
him alive, curse it for killing
his wife. He'd returned to retrieve
belongings and found himself afloat,
appropriated by the cold, voyeuristic
current that exploits every miracle.

Canoe
—*after Henri Vaillancourt*

All of us gone out of reach of change
—*Edward Thomas*

It was in September many years ago I paddled a birchbark canoe for the first
and only time. We had to let it soak before we launched, standing next to it
in the muddy shallows, leaning on the gunwales, making small talk as the tide
flooded in, the marsh grass held its breath for another dunking, and the fibers
of the hull began to register, to swell with the ocean's information.

A war canoe, wide, with pronounced, vertical bow and stern, it could carry at
least six, and you can only imagine how an object so relatively light responded
to so many people working to propel it, all bent to the task, calling out to
synchronize as we cleared the estuary into the empty bay where summer was
being repealed, and the current conceded, gave up discouraging our progress.

Now that we had found our peripheral rhythm, we stroked in silence, eyes
released from each other's arms and paddle blades to absorb the panorama,
almost a little disappointed no one was out there slamming along in a sleek
fiberglass outboard to witness this quiet anachronism prowling along the
deserted beach underneath the unraveling basket of Boston-bound contrails.

That early Autumn brilliance was suddenly upon me today, back again from
before our children, their marriages, their *own* children. How the sun was a hot
yoke across my shoulders. How that canoe grew more at home each second
spent riding the dip and surge of confused seawater, gradually recognizing
in that translucence a precarious blue language, some forgotten unratified
agreement. Is there a statute of limitations for buoyancy?

I haven't thought about that day so vividly since it happened. And I think I
understand it better now, appreciate more deliberately while hunkering in this
box of books, guitars, mementos and empty coffee cups my study has become,
how aware I was of being suspended by a tension from which I had been
estranged in every other boat. This one read the surface like braille, all flex

and accommodation; the rough husk had patience, bearing a band of clumsy
dilettante hijackers over deep trenches where they should have drowned. Under
my knees, the wet bark undulated between ribs as I stabbed the Atlantic and
drew (take *that*, and *that*), convinced I was hauling the salvaged hulk of someone
else's past to a new, safer harbor, not some anxious hungry part of myself

farther into the future. Do the implements of heritage (and, by association, longing) have an expiration date?

For two years, I'd seen it hanging parched, capsized, sullen as a sarcophagus in the rafters of my landlord's barn, dusted with decades of swallow down, bat guano, cairns of acorn caps and seed chaff arranged by wintering rodents. I visited it as you would a friend who's gravely ill, equivocating outside his door, fearing your presence might hurt him by reminding him of what you have, and what he is missing or stands to lose, as if, somehow, the value of his life had something to do with you.

Surface Fugue: Clark's Island, Wampanoag Bowl, *Carcharodon Carcharias*

> —but I saw
> Too far into the sea, where every maw
> The greater on the less feeds evermore.—
> But I saw too distinct into the core
> Of an eternal fierce destruction…
> *—John Keats, from a letter to J. H. Reynolds, March 25, 1818*

I.

There are no good synonyms for *predator*, really,
only names.
              I used to think the story
above sea level is always changing, always
invisible from underneath. You wouldn't have seen
the empty *wetus*, skeletal domes,
                              silences
of plague,
          or, now,
                    these landlocked squabbles between
the soon to be
              decommissioned nuke and turbines,
floral, sword-strokes of their stiff petals cashing
in on Plymouth's stiff offshore.
                              But fish
know the shapes they did back then:
                              mishoon,
then shallop (Clark tacking the bay, shaking
off December squalls). A boat from below
is under-
          belly, apex, maybe mammalian.

                              Herding
horizons of pogies, the bass gorge in summer,
inscribe with appetite their platinum ceiling around
my skiff.

          Among the boulders, almost boulders
themselves, "horsehead" seals, shoulder deep,

congregate, suspicious elders eyeing my idling,
forehead to temple with gossip,

                    prayers. Maybe
the propeller's rip and growl, the lingering wake's
unnatural

        slaps to their faces,

               or a glimpse of hull
that trips

        their blood's alert, survivalist wiring
getting the drift

          of some intention of teeth,
some pending penetration of colony, ballistic,
through gathering clouds

            of bunker.

                  A wave's wall
is the surface

        on its side. I remember
dragging a hand along it, as if to reach
through to seals on the other side surfing
side-by-side

        with me. We were poor
imitations in adjacent rooms, not
reflections. And to call them shadows won't
capture the braid of flippers and snouts defined
beyond my board's rail.

           The beach was a river
of white blowing sand, the water almost
ashen, and swells ahead of the hurricane arrived
through fog. The seals were hunting.

               Something,
probably, hunted them. And I was there
for fun.

II.

      Whatever name the locals had
for the island is someone else's

            memory of going
there, scuttled dugout, ferry of language
sunk somewhere between the Algonquin *monponsett,*
"at the deep clear space," and *munponsett,*

Wampanoag for "island
                    crossing place,"
                                        distinctions
extinguished like bootprint and rudder-rut in sand,
shifty as Saquish across the strait, that current-
jimmied door left open, breach that
let them in.

            In the foyer of the Historical
Society is the property of Metacom,
                                a man
they called King Philip: a vessel hewn
from burl—elm's deformity—hollowed bulb
of knots, cross-purposes
                            of branch and trunk,
with holes bored through the rim to loop
a leather thong he'd cinch around his waist
for wading lowbush blueberry, prizing quahogs
like easy confessions from the mud, or shim
between his knees for eating *samp*.
                                    The new
stewards stuffed it with ballots, decisions made
to keep their inheritance safe, from tool to trophy,
practicality to *objet:*
                    Don't mistake it
for a relic, holy and incarcerated in its cube
of glass, like a saint's purported mold and rags.

I understand a nation
                    and culture
are not at stake if someone kicks in
my door, murders me and my wife, steals
my favorite coffee cup or maple bowl
for salad (the only wedding gift
                            we kept),
dropped by children eager to help and seasoned
by the rule of never using soap,
                                decades
of oil, anchovies, garlic, avocado slush,
dinner after family dinner protected
in the house of its grain.

III.

                    In the Seychelles,
the giant trevally flies, swims fast
enough to leave the sea and wolf the flying
tern.
        Here, girls snapping pictures
of seals said the shark launched them upward,
vanished. They were out here
                        flailing
for capsized kayaks, fifteen minutes, fifteen-
foot animal beneath maybe banging
a U-ey for another go,
                    more
likely repelled by texture, acrid taste
of modernity. In the news clip ("I saw
four feet of its head…"), they're almost giddy
with the privilege of being
                        hit, giddy with
survival.

                    When the tide nabs me, engine
cut, past Bug Light's hydrant *solus*
rex beneath an August thunderhead,
I picture their plastic pods, tooth-embossed.
How do I appear
                to such resolution
rising to ravage, the visual calculus that converts
bow to nose, stern to tail?
                    Dialed-in
from the dashboard of its brain, I am
just another swimming piece of meat,
a body
        black and graspable against the sun,
enticing
        as a tangle of smoke above oaks,
spied from a mast.

                    Cocksure stalkers all,
gawkers on the fringe of instinct-
                        ual surgical theater
until we are
            the chain in action, oblivious
links.

Balancing
             on the prow, I ambushed schoolies
with line and lure, rooting for wing-storm, chaos
of gulls and gills bringing the surface to
a rapid boil
             of assault.
                    The fin I saw
across the moil's demolished mirror was darker
than the dawn's gelatinous gray, too planar
to be
      a dolphin's, more like a sail at home
in the air where I was casting
                          fate
                          to the wind,
extra-
      polating the outcomes of angling,
                                falling in,
being fished.
             All terrorists are amateurs.

$\int$

Notes

Champlain—Samuel de Champlain, 1574-1635

"Kalimérisma" (Distique du Bonjour)—Refers to a version sung by Ekaterini Mangoúlia, recorded in 1930 by Samuel Baud-Bovy (*Grece: Chansons et danses populaires*, Gallo, 1995), which artist Heiner Goebbels also recycled in his composition/installation and recording "Stifters Dinge" (ECM Records, 2012)

"Alas, the agony of citizenship is never ending."—Roger D. Hodge, from "Speak, Money" (*Harper's* magazine, October 2010)

"Cousteau..."—Jacques-Yves Cousteau, explorer, diver, conservationist, filmmaker, 1910-1997

"And yet, off alone, we were happy..."—Rainer Maria Rilke, from *Duino Elegies*. tr. Edward Snow (North Point Press, 2000)

"Crab Studies"—Inspired by Vincent Van Gogh's "Two Crabs" and "Crab On Its Back" (1888), and John Ruskin's "Study of a Velvet Crab" (c. 1870)

"Would now the wind..."—Herman Melville, from *Moby Dick*, Chapter 135, *The Chase.-Third Day*; (Arion Press/University of California Press, 1979)

"Weston..."—Edward Weston, photographer, 1886-1958; *"Lobos..."*—Point Lobos, Carmel-by-the-Sea, California; *"Antonioni..."*—Michelangelo Antonioni, film director, 1912-2007; *"Fellini..."*—Federico Fellini, film director, 1920-1993

Henri Vaillancourt—The New Hampshire-based builder of Abnaki and Algonquin canoes, who came to the wider public's attention as the subject of John McPhee's book, *The Survival of the Bark Canoe* (Farrar, Straus & Giroux, 1975). The craft described in this poem was built by Vaillancourt for Bob Bryan (1931-2018), founder of the Quebec Labrador Foundation and half of the Maine humor duo "Bert and I."

"Someone must watch..."—Franz Kafka, from *"At Night"; The Complete Stories* (Schocken, 1995)

"All of us..."—Edward Thomas, from "Haymaking" (Bloodaxe Books, 2008)

"Carcharodon Carcharias"—Genus and species, great white shark.

"...but I saw / Too far into the sea...."—John Keats, in a Letter to John Reynolds, March, 1818. *Selected Letters of John Keats* (Harvard University Press, 2002)

ACKNOWLEDGMENTS

Poems in this book have appeared in the following magazines, some in earlier versions:

The Adroit Journal: Crab Studies—"Libinia Emarginata (Common Spider Crab)"

Agni: "Elegy: Letter to My Wife's Grandfather, Canadian Artillery, 1917," "The Narrows: Lake George, 1969"

American Poetry Review: "Boys Riding Bicycles to School"

Birmingham Poetry Review: "Orient Point"

Crab Creek Review: "Tunnel, Regent's Canal"

Cutleaf: "The New Bathymetry," "Language," "Poem About Walden Pond Without Any Mention of Thoreau," "Skiff Hill"

Down East: "Frozen Boat"

Glassworks: Crab Studies—"Uca Pugnax (Fiddler Crab)"

Harvard Review: "Two Short Films of My Father"

Margie: The Journal of American Poetry: "Loss Prevention"

Memorious: "The Cigarette Wheel"

New England Review: "Surface Fugue: Clark's Island, Wampanoag Bowl, *Carcharodon Carcharias*" (Pushcart Prize nominee)

The New Formalist: "Elegy: Late August, Ipswich Bay," "Shipyard Aubade"

The New Republic: "An Azalea Blooms in the Murderer's Yard"

Ploughshares: "Fish Brook," "Driving Past the Properties I Landscaped as a Teenager"

POETRY: "Prayer as Bomb"

The Prague Revue: "Physical Fitness"

Salamander: "Bathers at White Horse Beach," "Refugees," "Triptych: Portrait at Fifteen with Dog Swimming in Foreground"

Sea Change: "Wind Indicators," "After the Shark"

The Southampton Review: "Giant Nazi Flag Escapes From an Attic Vodka Box"

Southwest Review: "Meditation"

Southern California Review (Exposition): "Children Driving"

Split Rock Review: "Canoe"

Zócalo Public Square: "Beach Walk, 1972," "Boys Playing Army in a Deserted Nursery," "San Fernando Valley, 1961," "Shinkawa's Problem"

THE AUTHOR WOULD LIKE TO THANK...

The editors at EastOver Press—Keith Lesmeister, Denton Loving, Kelly March and Walter Robinson—for rescue and anchorage after more than a decade of close calls, protean shapes and evaporating titles. Designer Kate Larken, for the book I imagined. Photographer Kenny Hurtado, for the perfect wave.

The following editors and writers for their belief in and/or direct connection to poems in this book: Jennifer Barber, Rick Barot, Nathaniel Bellows, Sven Birkerts, Sumita Chakraborty, Andrea Cohen, Maggie Dietz, Rebecca Morgan Frank, Crystal Gibbins, Major Jackson, Carolyn Kuebler, Peter LaBerge, Glyn Maxwell, Bill Pierce, Lynne Potts, Melanie Rehak, Elizabeth Scanlon, Julie Sheehan, Wilfred Spiegelman, Christina Thompson, Laura van den Berg, Adam Vines, Lou Ann Walker, and Christian Wiman.

David Huddle, for thirty-five years of banter, exacting criticism, patience, friendship. Michael Collier, whose encouragement and presence as a poet and teacher abide these poems.

The Water Street Bards—Todd Hearon, Matt Miller and Willie Perdomo—for the clean fuel of camaraderie, the mysterious balance of *work*, "work" and play.

The Sanctuaries: The American School in London, for the Bergeron Fellowship and subsequent pilgrimages, especially the kindness, generosity and hospitality of the locals—Miles Dunmore, Megan McGilchrist, Stephan Potchatek, Holly vanderMolen, and Kim Zeineddine. The Chubb-LifeAmerica Fellowship at MacDowell. Phillips Exeter Academy, for the gifts of sabbatical and professional development. Kieve-Wavus Education, for its generous support of the Damariscotta Lake Writers' Conference (2012-14), and the provision of time and space for teachers who write. Chris and Deirdre Caldarone for the life raft of Crooked Lane. Arthur and Sarah Evans, for The Bunkhouse—an enduring burrow and study like no other. Sarah and Ben Anderson at The Word Barn, a sublime local venue, oasis of language and music.

Jake and Jenny Sneeden/Madeleine and Tyler Page, for generous artistic refuge on the West Coast, aesthetic and experiential reconnection with the homeland from Del Mar Ave. to Walnut St., Ocean Beach to Ocean Beach, and the uncompromising supervision of Charlie the dachshund. The productive bunkers of Baja Brent and Eddie Ortiz.

My students, whose discussions have enlarged and fortified my commitment to reading and writing, whose dependable daily hunger has intensified my own.

Paul Yoon and Laura van den Berg, for their friendship and their example of unrelenting devotion to the written word. Ellen Bryant Voigt, friend and force, always.

CPSIA information can be obtained
at www.ICGtesting.com
Printed in the USA
LVHW101458140922
728371LV00017B/461/J

9 781934 894668